Rub Your Nose
Meow Like A Cat
Shake Your Tail

Helpers Oath

I am a silly cat and promise to do

EVERYTHING

{readers name} successfully reads from within this book.

Meow, Meow, Meow.

My helper will

Clap
3
times.

My helper will

Hop like a
bunny.

My helper will Rub their nose when I say Blue.

My helper will Catnap!

Blue,

blue,

Blue,

blue,

My helper will

WAKE UP.

My helper will

Walk like a cat.

My helper will Meow when I say yellow.

My helper will

Purrrrr

Blue, yellow, blue, yellow.

My helper will

Tell me
a joke.

My helper will

Shake their tail when I say green.

Blue,
yellow,
green,
yellow.

Green,
green,
green,
green.

My helper will Jump 3 times and yellow.

My helper will

Lay on
the floor.

Yellow, Blue, Yellow.

My helper will

Dance.

My helper will

Chase

their tail.

Green,

yellow,

green,

yellow.

My helper

Is a silly
cat

My helper

 free

from their

oath

Did you enjoy this book? Please leave us a review

Rub Your Nose
Meow Like A Cat
Shake Your Tail

Claw Here
Rub Your Nose
Meow Like A Cat
Shake Your Tail

Ingram Content Group UK Ltd.
Milton Keynes UK
UKHW051909260423
420851UK00002B/28